THE WHITE SPARK

A New Book, giving out a New Philosophy and the Mysteries of the Universe

The Handbook of the Millennium and the New Dispensation

By
ORVILLE LIVINGSTON LEACH

Revised and Edited By
Dennis Logan
[2021]

Copyright 2021 by Rolled Scroll Publishing
ISBN: 9781952900402

SYNOPSIS OF CONTENTS

This book is called The White Spark as the white spark or vacuum cell in Nature IS THE RIGHT HAND OF GOD—it is a ubiquitous principle of the universe and is the cause and parent of electricity, combustion, radium, snow-flakes, flowers, trees, leaves, crystallization, wireless telegraphy, animal forms and EVEN LIFE ITSELF.

This book is the key to every department of human endeavor, as it enunciates the basic principle and THE PRIME MOVER of the universe.

It tells the road to health, the cause and cure of disease, the truth about the germ humbug and drug treatments, serums and antitoxins.

It shows why luminosity is produced on the flesh of various organisms, why a slice of pollock when first iced, then heated to 100 degrees and then thrust into a temperature of 50 degrees becomes luminous.

It shows the farmer that he can become a magician of agriculture—tells that the nitrogen of the air is only a dust of quartz rocks, like the invisible moisture of the air is "a dust of water"—that the nodules on the roots of the clover and legumes do not abstract nitrogen from the air, for if they did nature would have placed these bacteriological growths on the vine and not the root, the scientists have the cart before the horse in this case and the nodular cells form the proteins from sand or silica, this book tells how it is done.

It tells what a trance is and how the soul can leave the body temporarily.

How JESUS CHRIST is carrying out the biblical prophesy by TELEPATHY.

Gives the truths about the ideal society, alcohol, drunkenness, causes of crime, longevity and law.

It shows why milk from the cow at 100 degrees of temperature if suddenly cooled to 50 degrees by the small stream process will keep long and remain free from bacteria—how radioactivity kills the germs of fermentation and prevents ptomaine poisoning and why out door livers or moderately working farmers are the centenarians.

Gives the statistics to prove the evils of alcohol and fast living.

Shows that all force even gravity is a radioactive emanation from the white sparks and that universal gravitation is a vagary, that the planets move on orbits which are RIBBONS OF FORCE like the gulf stream.

The author is the man who converted the great scientists to the idea that matter was simply "A HOLE IN THE ETHER" and that the ether was the real and only element in the universe.

This proves the truth of the biblical statement, that God made the world out of nothing, and that matter is simply spirit in motion.

This book shows how all the conditions of crime react upon us, that physiology and rectitude are interdependent and although you do not go to hell, yet hell will come to you if you transgress the laws of God and Nature.

It shows the power of mind over the body and that the religion of Jesus is not a fluke to satisfy a whim but is a great commercial like business. There is no vicarious atonement in Nature, She does not bandy and has no favorites, you get what you pay for, She keeps no books but has an automatic adjustment which regulates accounts as you go along and marks your soul for the future as well.

This book advocates churches and pastors or teachers who are God's Noblemen and it advocates THEOCRATIC DEMOCRACY for if you love God and your neighbor you are the CORRECT LAW.

But you can never overrule the law that your temper, rage, cruelty and vindictiveness will be uncontrollable as long as you use tobacco, alcohol and meats, and WAR WILL NOT BE ANNIHILATED UNTIL YOU REFORM YOUR DIET AND HABITS. "Abstinence begets spirituality—dissipation crime", and yourself, your wife, children, associates, animals and humanity suffer—you have misapprehensions, moroseness and misery.

War is the result of selfishness, greed, graft, ignorance and animalism and it advocates education of the individual to the end that he shall combine and amalgamate his power with his fellow citizen, when he can control WAR and government.

This book shows that diffusion of light and the freezing of water into ice is from one white spark radiating "high frequency" straight cold rays against its warm neighboring molecule and causing it to become a white spark itself, it gives "contagion," it shows that the ether or spirit gives "contagious transmission of ideas."

It explains MONISM as being correct and that there is but one God.

It explains that all of the material of a combustive nature Naturally is censored by going to the intestines, and here it is emulsified and coated with an incombustive coat of albumen, if an oil and if starch is turned into sugar which in turn is changed to an oily substance in the liver later and this is subsequently emulsified for eligibility to the blood, but alcohol, essential oils and the organic bases sneak into the blood surreptitiously, therefore "medicine" is not food, there may be times when a stimulant is a pathological aid and the germs often make a stimulant in the body to help over a bad condition, as when the system contains useless material which is a load on the organs or when minerals or "humors" embalm the system, but only a limited amount is a medicine, any more is a poison, these cases are anomalies and under proper conditions are transgressions of Nature.

This book shows that we can live upon a few cents per day and be stronger and better in every way—it shows why many who gave up eating meat failed and how they can discard the evil and cease to make graveyards of their stomachs—the author has experimented with dogs and cats and found that by feeding milk and well cooked oat-meal from the weaning period till maturity they throve and were happier gentler and more active and vivacious.

Meat causes man to be peevish, ill tempered and criminal, like tobacco, alcohol and drugs.

The differentiation of animal bodies can be met by the cooking of the cereals, the short intestines and other conditions of carnivorous animals are not inhibitions to the discarding of meat as a food.

Man and animals require pure soft water, hard and polluted water is a cause of much unsuspected poisoning and the hidden cause of "epidemics" and diseases—all water should be analyzed before being accepted as satisfactory.

Mineralized waters are not desirable and the waters from some wells and springs are fit for plants but will disorder the liver and constipate the bowels—many farms are in the grip of misfortune and losses from having bad water for the use of the home and the animals.

All of the unused elements which are thrown into the large intestine as waste should be discharged regularly and in cases of constipation a mild laxative like Cascara Sagrada or Senna should be taken to help Nature.

The great category of medicines of the doctors is a farce and there is no mysterious "selective affinity" for certain drugs, but all elements have either one of two actions—a stimulating process or a refrigerating or embalming process, some remedies go to the liver and counteract the embalming action and aid the flow of bile and some may be of a resinous nature and saponify in the alkalies of the intestines and aid their action.

It will be seen that the book simplifies medicine to **TWO PRINCIPLES**, one counteracting the other like heat and cold but these actions are unnatural and undesirable; it is only by avoiding discrepancies and ameliorations that we follow Nature.

The book explains that the differentiations and forms in the universe are the results of two forces, the curved force and the straight force, just the same as every word in English language is made up of letters having only two kinds of lines, the straight and the curved lines. The book tells just what occurs in the life cells and protoplasm; this is a remarkable discovery and to show how much so, we quote from Le Bon the great Scientist, he says: "THE SCHOLAR CAPABLE OF SOLVING BY HIS INTELLIGENCE THE PROBLEMS SOLVED EVERY MOMENT BY THE CELLS OF THE LOWEST CREATURE WOULD BE SO MUCH HIGHER THAN OTHER MEN THAT HE MIGHT BE CONSIDERED BY THEM AS A GOD." (From EVOLUTION OF FORCES, p. 363).

Haeckel declared that a cell did not go to the bottom of the secret of life and that we must allow that the naked protoplasm itself held the secret of life, this book proves that protoplasm is composed of molecules with centers of sulphur and phosphorus which conformed into WHITE SPARKS by the alternations of heat and cold, the SPARKS contain spirit and each spark has a quiet center or consciousness and a potential of radiation of force.

This book is terse and compact, is printed on good paper and bound with red cloth with gold letters.

READ IT!

THEN TELL YOUR NEIGHBORS ABOUT IT

The White Spark

Part First.

This work is an exposition of a NEW PHILOSOPHY, and although it has been taught to a number of highly educated men,—in a technical way, we have had many suggestions made to us to publish a work which the "work-a-day" people can understand,—some have said: "It is too far above me," and "why don't you explain it so everybody may understand it."

In this section we have especially planned to overcome all such incongruities.

First of all we want to say that nature is a strict economist of time, material and energy—her acts and laws are the simplest possible.

When you see any philosophy that is complicated, it is wrong, but if it teaches simplicity it is right—the orthodox creeds have maintained that the universe contained two distinct and eternal elements—MATERIAL AND SPIRIT—but this is complication—can be reduced,—WE ARE MONISTS AND "PANTHEISTS" and we are right,—there is ONLY ONE ELEMENT IN THE UNIVERSE, AND THAT IS THE PRISTINE SPIRIT.

This is all that is needed to form the universe, and we will show that matter is simply an enclosure of SPACE or nothing, having an outline of spirit which is in such swift motion that it holds the outline—water can be sent through the air so swiftly that it will turn aside a steel bar.

To better illustrate the fact we will take a blackboard and paint it all over with whitewash, then we take a wet sponge and wipe out round figures—these will show as black spaces outlined by the white—these black spaces represent SPACE or nothing, while the white represent SPIRIT—the black spots then represent MATTER. They are really nothing, only a form outlined and held by motion of spirit or "ETHER."

The statement in catechisms that "GOD MADE THE WORLD OUT OF NOTHING" is then correct, although the statement has been called impossible by many scientists.

Our philosophy was the first to enunciate the true nature of matter, atoms, molecules and electrons. Previous to this atoms were considered as solid indivisible particles. Later the scientists said matter was condensed spirit or ether. I imagined so myself once, but upon reflection I said, "THE ETHER CAN PASS THROUGH EVERYTHING, SO WHAT COULD HOLD IT OR COMPRESS IT?" And spirit or ether could not compress ether, as ether is all alike.

To show our part in teaching the world the truth we will go into a little history.

As the readers of this work have probably never read THE LATCH KEY, I will reprint two paragraphs verbatim, numbers 6 and 17.

Paragraph 6 will require some explanation. Count Rumford claimed that heat was nothing but a motion, and in some cases this is so, a motion of the atoms in a body, but a line of spirit from the sun will cause atoms on the earth to move, and thus is the real cause of heat, and so radiation of force or spirit from burning wood will create heat. Perhaps we have in this paragraph used the nature of spirit rather vaguely in saying heat is the "prime mover," but heat in one way is spirit, or analogous to spirit.

6.
Matter Is Only Space or Nothing, With a Wall of Spirit.

Fire was held in sublime awe by the Egyptians and the sun was worshipped as the source of Divine Power. The wonderful Pyramids are supposed to have been erected for the glorification of these subtle forces in Nature.

Modern thought reverts to ancient ideas.

Fire is simply spirit in motion.

Heat is a circular or circumscribed motion or **direction** in which spirit is moving—it is the "Prime Mover" of organization, the creator of matter and the parent of the universe!

A centrifugal act occurring from the intellectual fiat of spirit—leaving a center, a whirling away of spirit to a certain circumference or distance from a center leaving space in the center—this is materialization, a creating of matter, the formation of an atom, from nothing!

17.

The Point of a Pin Illustrates the Annihilation of Matter.

A point continued to an absolute end must end in spirit! Matter is cut down to something beyond our senses; the absolute end of a point may contain an atom, but matter ends here—here where one single whirl of spirit surrounds the smallest amount of space possible. Beyond there is no whirl or motion of spirit, consequently no matter, yet there is now un-particled spirit.

If electricity had been studied correctly no scientist would ever have imagined that matter was condensed ether. In Maxwell's Elementary Treatise on Electricity on page 49 he says: "WE KNOW ABSOLUTELY NOTHING WITH RESPECT TO THE DISTANCE THROUGH WHICH ANY PARTICULAR PORTION OF ELECTRICITY IS DISPLACED FROM ITS ORIGINAL POSITION." * * * "THE ACTUAL

VELOCITY OF ELECTRICITY IN A TELEGRAPH WIRE MAY BE VERY SMALL, LESS, SAY, THAN THE HUNDREDTHS OF AN INCH IN AN HOUR, THOUGH THE SIGNALS WHICH IT TRANSMITS MAY BE PROPAGATED WITH GREAT VELOCITY."

It is the very fact that the ether is not compressible that allows a wireless signal to be given a thousand miles away instantly. It is just the same as if you had a long stick and punched a bell 20 feet away.

I sent my work, "The Latch Key," to Sir Oliver Lodge and Sir William Crookes in 1904. Its philosophy was buried for three years before the ideas were presented to the British Association for the Advancement of Science.

Sir William Crookes wrote to me in 1904 stating that he had received my pamphlet, but he was just leaving home for a vacation of two weeks and when he returned he would give it his attention.

In Sir Oliver's great work, called "Life and Matter," he wrote: "But it appears now that an atom may break up into electric charges, and these again may some day be found capable of resolving themselves into pristine ether. In that case the ether alone persists. It is the most fundamental entity."

In another book called "Modern Views of Electricity" he said: "Ether is somehow affected by the immediate neighborhood of gross matter, and it appears to be **concentrated** inside it to an extent depending on the **density** of the matter."

So it is seen that Sir Oliver at this time believed that matter was compressed or condensed ether.

In my pamphlets I explained that the ether could not be compressed, as it was capable of passing through all substance, and that matter was not **more** of the ether, but instead was **less,** and that atoms were simply spots of pure space or "nothing," and that the ether or its moving lines or sheets simply whirled around on empty space while what was called a vacuum was really the habitat of real material, or the ether.

In 1907 Sir Oliver accepted this new version of the nature of matter, and it was the cause of much excitement in the British Association, so much so that the report reached America and Prof. Serviss wrote an article about it in the Boston Sunday American in October, 1907, in which he says: "The answer as recently given by Sir Oliver Lodge is amazing beyond belief. The solidest thing in existence, he avers, is the very thing which for generations has been universally regarded as the lightest, the most imperceptible, the most utterly tenuous and evanescent beyond all definition or computation—the ether!" And in the same article he says: "Matter, Prof. Osborne Reynolds has asserted, instead of being, as we innocently believe on the evidence of our senses, the only real and solid thing in nature is, in fact, the absence or deficiency of mass."

The following is an article by Sir Oliver Lodge in regard to spirits:

"Though for many years, ever since the eighties, I have tried all sorts of other methods of explaining these things, they have gradually been eliminated one after the other, and now no explanations remain except the simple one that the people who communicate are really the individuals they claim to be. Not always, of course. One has to prove them in every case. But still the conclusion is that survival of existence can be scientifically proved by actual psychical investigation.

"That all leads to a perception of the unity running through all states of existence. That is why I say that man is not alone; that is why I say that I know he is surrounded by other intelligences. If you once step over the boundary beyond man, there is no limit to higher and higher intelligences up to the Infinite Intelligence himself. There is no stopping; you go on and must go on until you come to God.

"It is no strange land to which I am leading you. The Cosmos is one. We here on this planet are limited in certain ways and are blind to much that is going on; but I tell you we are surrounded by beings working with us, cooperating, helping such as people in visions have had some perception of. And that which religion tells us, that saints and angels are with us, that the Master Himself is helping us, is, I believe, literally true."

In presenting this work to the public we claim no right to inject any fallacies into the mind of the reader, and as far as we can discover there is no cause for any misapprehension in regard to our statements. THERE IS ONLY ONE TRUTH to any question, and all we base our claims upon is our ability to present facts pertaining to our enunciations.

Fallacies are very short lived among persons who use their brains, and the only credit which any philosophy earns is from the good precepts which it inculcates, the value which it proves to the world and the TRUTH WHICH IT HOLDS.

It is usually the case that a careless person resents any philosophy which conflicts with their habits, no matter how many facts you present to them or how much history you cite to them in proof of your statements.

The use of tobacco and liquor deadens the users' alertness to safeguarding their own welfare, and in many cases with poisons and also diet the only thing we can do is to try to have you learn the truth, and if the end of the rope has been reached and you are at the ebb of life and hope, you will have more willingness to conform to the laws of life. If you don't need our philosophy as a "missionary," some time, you may want it as a doctor. Learn it, anyway.

The greatest field for fruitful efforts is with the children. If we can prevent their using improper articles of food and drink and teach them the nature of their effects, then we may find better soil for the seeds of rectitude. Of course a little dissipation may not always cause great trouble.

There is but ONE GOD and we may tell about SAVIOURS, "SONS OF GOD" and the TRINITY, but there is only one SAVIOUR and that is A TEACHER—either a SPIRIT or a HUMAN BEING—and the only salvation is in the following of Natural Laws which are GOD'S BIBLE. There are Natural laws which are OCCULT LAWS, and these sometimes contravene what we may call "LAWS OF MATTER."

A TEACHER OF THE TRUTHS OF NATURAL SCIENCE IS GOD'S NOBLEMAN, and KNOWLEDGE IS OUR ONLY SALVATION.

The use of stimulants is just the same as if you should use a 104 volt electric lamp on a current with 250 volts. It would be burnt out; and so your nerves which are the wires of the body are wasted away by stimulants. They are all alike practically. Alcohol and essential oils act as a kindler to the natural combustives in the tissues and the alkaloids or organic bases, as nicotine, morphine, etc., act like radium.

Quinine is an alkaloid also, and I will here reprint a selection from the original LATCH KEY which explains the manner in which the organic bases become dangerous. They all contain nitrogen, which may account for their affinity for the nerve substance.

32.
Light and Heat From Radium Are From the Absorption of Ether.

The emission of light from a substance spontaneously, as in the case of "Radium," is not a new phenomenon. Nearly forty years ago Prof. Stokes enunciated the fact.

He filled a glass tube with a solution of sulphate of quinine and then moved it through the spectrum, entering at the red ray. When it had passed through all the colors and entered the region of the ultra violet, or where the invisible magnetic rays were, the tube lighted up.

A solution of horse chestnut acted in the same way, so also did glass stained with oxide of uranium.

Paragraph 45 was sort of a mysterious alchemical article explaining a secret of life. Life comes from the formation of WHITE SPARKS or vacuo in matter, and therefore bioplasmic elements MUST BE LIQUID, SOLUBLE OR MOBILE. They must be capable of conforming into ROUND GLOBULES. Then the second feature must come in—heat and cold to expand the molecule and cool the outside and allow the inside to later contract and form a vacuum in the center, the home of SPIRIT.

"Decay" generates life as it makes solid substances soluble. Of course, excessive decay creates a gas and then this evaporates.

45.

Secrets of Silicon.

Moses was a great alchemist, skilled in all the arts and sciences of the Egyptians. The works or writings of Moses are called Books of the Old Testament and not works on alchemy, but tradition tells us that his sister Miriam wrote an extensive work on alchemy—(the Catholic Bible has the name Miriam translated as Mary).

In Genesis Chap. 3, verse 19, we read, "Till thou return unto the ground, for out of it thou was taken; for dust thou art and unto dust shalt thou return."

Some scientists scoff at the idea of Moses and some scoff at the idea of "Spontaneous Generation," but we can prove that both are true.

Life can be produced from MINERAL ELEMENTS ALONE.

Silicon has always been a source of dispute among chemists in regard to its classification. Some consider it a regular metal, but it is usually called a "hyalogen" or glass former like Boron.

Silicon is never found in its pure metallic state in nature, but is in combination with oxygen, as is then called by various names as Silica, Silex, Silicic Acid and SAND, which is the most abundant of mineral substances.

The most important and useful elements as air, water and sand God gives FREE TO ALL, they are found everywhere.

Sand is at one time a crystallized substance and at another time it may be A COLLOID substance and thus become the same nature as an "organized substance," as albumen.

Sand is insoluble in pure water, but it is dissolved by alkaline solutions. Natural waters which contain alkaline carbonates always have some sand in solution.

Sand from its two fold nature seems to be the bond between death and life or the solution to the theory of "from dust to life."

Sand when in solution is a colloid.

If 8 or 10 parts of carbonate of soda or potash are mixed with 12 or 15 parts of sand and 1 part of charcoal on being heated they melt and form a mass resembling ordinary glass, but it entirely dissolves in **hot water.**

If now chlorohydric acid be added to the solution it neutralizes the alkali and the silica or sand separates as A TRANSPARENT JELLY. A colloid! It is "hydrate of silica," but it is now fixed like albumen or an organized substance and is insoluble in water or acid.

If it is kept moist it remains a colloid, but by drying it and separating it from its partner, water, the colloid making alchemical mysterious WATER, the sand turns to dust again—a gritty powder!

At common temperatures carbonic acid is stronger than silica, and upon many of the combinations of silica the air acts as a destructive agent, its carbonic acid slowly uniting with bases or alkali and liberating the silica, and at the moment of its liberation the sand is soluble in water.

Sand, it will be seen, acts both as an acid and combines with an alkali and as a base and combines with acids.

Sand in solution enters the roots of plants and from its transforming nature or transmutation, it performs great wonders in nature, it performs miracles in the animal body and in water itself.

It is the ideal agent for the generation of **vacuo spaces** or life cells, from its being in one state when warm and in another when cold, from its being capable of forming soft cell walls and then concreting around a quantity of ether or spirit upon cooling. It proves itself the "Philosopher's Stone."

Hot and cold and silicon! What a wonderful combination! It explains the mysteries of the universe, radio-activity and life.

It may be well to here state that there is no chemical difference between a dead man's brain and nerves and a live man's brain and nerves. This in itself shows that the cause of life and intelligence is simply from some conformation of matter which allows the presence of Spirit. This is the invisible process of the formation of WHITE SPARKS or the making of a hollow center to molecules.

LIFE is not a principle per se of organic matter, but organic matter is arranged into round molecules with cell center of silicon phosphorus, sulphur or iron.

The hard and fast nature of the elements is an imagination and it is only a short step of nature from quartz or silicon to carbon and I may also say to nitrogen the gas of the atmosphere.

THE FARMER CAN BECOME A MAGICIAN by intellect. We once proved that by the use of lime or an alkali vegetables can be made to grow IN SAND. A tomato plant was planted in a mixture of sand and plasterer's mortar (a mixture of quick lime and sand) and a bushel of tomatoes were gathered from this one plant. The lime makes the sand soluble and acts the same as manure which produces carbonic acid which at the moment of its formation acts as a solvent of sand and this gives growth. Water is the great element of life and growth—with the heating effect of the sun and the alternations of temperature or cooling after heating we augment the life and growth.

I will reprint some more of the articles which were in THE LATCH KEY, as they seemed to strike the readers more impressibly than anything which I ever wrote, and in fact THE LATCH KEY seemed to have hypnotic influence. First of all IT WAS

ANONYMOUS and no author's name appeared and further it was given away.

One lady in later years found out the author and wrote to me for a few copies, saying she could not help crying when she read paragraph 37. Perhaps the paragraph took on the "poetical" and thus reached her sentiments.

37.
The Secret of Life!

The little chapel peacefully resting under the overhanging trees, with the solemn graveyard beside it, tells the story of life's longings and miseries. Yet within the little chapel, however humble, can be learned the secret of life's joy and success and the eternal happiness of the soul!

Life's sentiments are fragrant, space only is fraught with pain!

Spirit fledges space, unlocks the caverns of misery and sheds the light in the gloom.

Man grovels in the dark mid the skulls of despair till he lists to the whisper of spirit. The lisping pines, the rustling oaks, the sunshine in the meadow and the moonlight on the hill speak in accents calm and clear. Our motto:

"SPIRITUS EXCELLO."

Water is the great agent of life or conformation as it is mobile.

Molecules which are round when whirled or heated take to orbits, but the metallic substances having molecules of a disc shape whirl on their axes. I herewith give articles 26 and 42 of the LATCH KEY:

42.

Why Ashes or Water Do Not Burn.

Fire is the action of atoms or molecules in separating farther apart. To be sure, ashes have atoms, but for atoms to whirl apart their motion must be so that they can separate. If the heat causes them to whirl on their axis only, the substance may get red hot, but will not burn.

And some substances do not burn because the heat and motion applied whirls the molecules or groups of atoms apart and wastes its motion in that way. Water acts this way (steam).

Crystallization is the result of the formation of vaco cells or white sparks, and I reprint paragraph 26 to explain this fact:

26.

Annealing and Malleability of Metals.

Crystallization has been considered in paragraph 21, but when matter is cooled very slowly through long periods of time, vacuo spaces are not formed.

Ordinary cast iron is crystallized, but when it is heated in a furnace and gradually cooled through several days or weeks, it becomes "malleable iron."

The iron which is used as an electro-magnet for a telegraphic machine will not work unless the iron is annealed very soft by being heated and allowed to cool in the ashes as the fire gradually dies out.

Crystallization is the most wonderful dovetailing process conceivable. When a liquid is cooled the molecules become radio active and radiate lines of force. These lines are nearly straight, unlike heat lines, and therefore they are cold lines. They drive matter in planes and straight lines or surfaces instead of into globules or liquids which move. The discs of ice cannot move or roll about like the globules of water, and ice is hard like quartz or a form of flint or silica.

All objects are formed by the action of TWO forces, either a curling force or a straight force. Plants form leaves in the air, and where there is more obstruction and curving influence they form roots. ALL CELLS ARE ALIKE in their first state, but are changed in the process of growth or from influences.

A slip from a geranium when stuck into the earth will form roots. It seems to me that each cell in an egg contains a counterpart of the whole body of a chicken—that is, it contains electrons or occult matter which, once having passed through all parts of a fowl's body, in the blood photographs these parts.

We can account for the various parts of the egg yolk turning its cells into different forms by the location which the particular cell occupies—as cells in various parts,—at the center,—or at the surface,—would be subject to curling forces or straight forces. At the center forces would be obstructed and curled, and at the surface just the opposite, and a hundred variations, according to the location and surroundings.

How many times I have wished that a social condition could be instituted by which EVERY LIVING BEING in the world or the universe could be happy and free from fear, worriment, hunger, and exposure—where peace, plenty and pleasure existed for all—where all could have a horse, automobile, golf link or any correct thing which their ideas called for to make them enjoy themselves.

FOUR HOURS' labor per day is enough for any one and there is enough in the world to give every one happiness and plenty if THE SOCIAL CONDITION was arranged correctly.

While there are many unfeeling capitalists, yet the poor are not always right. They don't know how to act for their own welfare. They may know what they want, but don't know how to get it. An ignorant poor man will often sell his vote or he is too ignorant to learn that he should obey correct laws.

The London Spectator recently gave a biography of former Secretary of State JOHN HAY and I give an excerpt from the same:

"It was natural that Hay should despise the arts of the demagogue. He speaks with scorn of what he calls 'gutter Ciceros,' and of the practice adopted during a sharp electoral campaign of 'hiring dirty orators by the dozen to blather on street corners.' He very rightly held that it was the special duty of statesmen in democratic countries to have the courage of their opinions. He himself wrote a novel, entitled 'The Bread Winners,' which was widely read, and which was really an elaborate defense of capital against the attacks of labor; and in 1905 he wrote to President Roosevelt: 'It is a comfort to see the most popular man in America telling the truth to our masters, the people. It requires no courage to attack wealth and power, but to remind the masses that they too are subject to the law is something few public men dare to do.'

"America at her best can produce men of a very high type. Such a man was John Hay."

Part Second

Spirits and the Spirit Land.

1. Reveries in the Country.

It was a day in January. The desultory snow-flakes were skudding here and there and a white mantle was becoming visible on the fence tops and pine trees, and as I gazed dreamily from the window of my study I heard the church bell in the belfry of the village church peal out its glad tidings of love; and as its decadence faded away, a thought peaceful and quiet captured my soul,—it seemed as if the reverberating voice of the holy bell had told me a story—a secret of happiness and peace.

2. Redemption of the World.

And as I settled back in my broad wicker arm chair before the blazing hearth fire I said to my inner soul: "How beautiful is this moment! Can I perpetuate the sentiments which give me joy on this Sabbath day, can

I delve into the laws of comfort and rest and emerge with a TROPHY TO REDEEM THE WORLD?"

3. Spirit and Matter.

The scintillating sparks in the fireplace rose up on the wings of a golden glow, paused for a moment and then I saw a flash of pure white light gleam like the star of Bethlehem. I had seen the wild, red coals changed to peaceful, redeemed souls of light.

4. A Truism of Nature an Eternal Principle.

The church bell, emblematic of religion, and the "white spark," a ubiquitous principle of the universe; visions of the superstructure of the millennium, rose up before me—religion and science hand in hand, science the fact and religion the herald or harbinger.

5. Matter Only the Wake of Spirit.

I had seen that from out the depths of the base matter come forth a substance pure and glorious.

Transmutation then had proved that there is no vile, low or corrupt matter in the universe, and the idea is a relic of the ignorance inculcated in the dim vistas of the past. All matter is simply a figure sculptured by the pencil of spirit, vortices which use space as a playground, speed which holds the lines stiff and refractory against ultra intrusion.

6. Science of the White Spark.

Now I see two visions—two houses in the precinct of nature—the first a structure of spirit for the abode of space or nothing; second, a structure of space for the abode of spirit, the all, the great, the powerful, and the conscious; the first, a minute affair, an atom; the second, a collocation of atoms forming a shell or larger structure for the abode of spirit, and this is formed by a heated or mobile, molecule conforming substance, suddenly cooled by oxygen or a cold temperature, when a shell is formed and indurated, and a hollow center made.

7. Symbol of the White Spark.

I introduce a new symbol ° the emblem which will represent the white spark, the circle or hollow globe, for this is what the white spark is, and this spark prevails throughout the universe. It is a hollow molecule, holding an air-tight reservoir, excluding everything but spirit or the ether.

8. The Spark is a Receptacle of Mind and a Potential of Force.

The white spark is alive. It has a shell formed of rotating atoms which roll in the spirit or magnetic lines of force. The lines converge to a common center. Here they must halt for an instant. Force cannot be lost, so it is transmuted into consciousness. This mind can now radiate lines of force from the center out again.

9. Mathematics of the Spark.

If you take a silver dime and lay it on the table you will find that it always takes just six dimes to form a ring around it. This leaves six spaces between the dimes, and it is the same with atoms, and a molecule seen from the side if radio-active, and if we could see the lines of force, would show six streams of force, and the snow-flake always has six points.

10. Crumbling Sparks and Permanent Sparks.

The sparks of combustion explode from the inner force, but the "sparks" of a magnet and radium do not, and the sparks formed in protoplasm or in the nerves and brain last longer than the sparks of combustion, and the sparks in the spiritual bodies of departed souls are like radium.

11. Location of the Spirit Land.

In paragraph 6 I refer to two visions of houses in the precinct of nature. Now I refer to a third, the greatest, most beautiful and wonderful abode in the universe. This house has no interior of simple space or nothing, and again it has no outer wall of matter. It is the pristine spirit and it is in the interstellar spaces outside of the planets.

12. Conditions in the Spirit Land.

In this land there is no gravity or obstruction. What is built and placed there is free from destruction and decay. Living spirits can move by a thought and build by their desires; spirits can outstrip the earth in its flight in its orbit, can come to earth and leave at any time or part of its orbit. This is a home of joy.

13. Attributes of Spirit.

The soul is kept in our body by the magnetism of our blood. When a person goes into a trance there is an embargo on the blood and the soul can leave the spark cells of the nerve substance of the brain and occupy a spiritual body or electrical vapor in the atmosphere or ether. During sleep or failing powers of the mind, the soul is drowned out by matter, the permanent spiritual center of the spark is overflowed with matter and consciousness is temporarily turned to motion. Spirit always, in any amount, has the attributes of intelligence and power; the ether transmits intelligences.

14. Superiority of Spirit.

When our soul leaves our body it enters its own, it becomes clear and bright as in childhood; there is no fear, pain or dimness of thought and mind. We meet our friends, we remember and visit our earthly friends in the human body, we strive for their uplift and happiness, we live in happiness and peace, yet our earthly career affects our degree of spiritual advancement, and the truths which you can learn at the little country chapel and the emulation of the "SERMON ON THE MOUNT" will prove to be your "WAND OF HOPE."

15. The Pope Says the Advent of the Saviour Is Near.

In a decree of Pope Benedict sent out from Rome on January 19, 1915, he says: "Those days which Christ predicted seem in fact to have come, 'You shall hear of wars and rumors of wars. For nation shall rise against nation and kingdom against kingdom'." Christ can return to earth in spirit. There is no need for Him to come otherwise. He can talk to a person adapted to receive telepathic instructions and give the world His message.

Some readers may be averse to the claims that Jesus Christ is anything but an imaginary person from the inventions of the priests of the early ages, and others may claim that contemporary with the dates applied to the fictitious legend there was a great teacher and the teachings recorded were from this teacher. But what difference does a name make? The only issue of any value is what is taught. No great teacher cares a whit about what the people think about his personality if they accept his works. The name Jesus has been applied to the teacher of the good things in the New Testament for so long a time now that we can well afford to grant the application, whatever might have been his acceded name.

All the ether in interstellar space is intelligent, and if we connect our mind with it we gain power and intuition by a "sixth sense," but to do this we must not throw the blanket of too much blood about the brain. "Prophets" have to diet and fast.

Part Third

How to Generate the White Spark or "Vaco-Cells" in Our Body.

All the life and thought on this earth and in any material and on any other earth or body in the universe comes from a peculiar transaction by which all matter is cleared away and a space left wherein there is nothing but the invisible ether or spirit.

The origination of all tangible matter was from the degradation of spirit and the transmutation of thought into motion, and it is by the motion of spirit that matter is formed from spirit.

Therefore to regain the conditions of thought and to regulate the adjustment of material or matter conditions must be instituted which simulate the original state, and evade the decadence from contiguosity of matter and generate SPIRIT in vaco-cells with life and power.

This great principle is the keynote of all that we hope for in existence. It is the most vital science and yet it has remained totally hidden from the ken of mankind.

This NEW SCIENCE opens up a field in the new order which holds the greatest hopes for utopian success ever given to man.

It is not gold, power, notoriety or glamor that make for this great process of joy and health. It is not the costly foods and luxuries which bring us within reach of this coveted condition.

When we learn the facts we find that the great part of mankind are very much misinformed and that human knowledge is upside down. We find that peace and happiness like air and water are not under a ban, but that God is on the side of the unostentatious and simple living people, and that what has been considered by some as poverty is really greatness in disguise.

Nature never places any premium on truth and like all good things should be free of access.

Among the things which we give, you will find new methods of combatting disease, a means of economic freedom and of rising above misfortune.

We will show that most diseases are caused by the food and drink which is used. The theories of the "howling germ doctors" are all insane emanations from an ignorant mind. We will prove that there are two distinct types of disease with an admixture of these two types.

The first type is malarial and is caused by a mal-assimilation of sugar and grease, fat or oil in the system. The second type is "small-pox" and is caused by the non-assimilation of the nitrogenized element of meat, or gelatinous elements.

When you know the cause you can avoid the disease. GERMS or MICROBES are not the cause of disease, but are beneficent provisions of nature to reduce meat proteins, etc., which are blocking the system, to a state in which they can be eliminated from the blood, and therefore we always find the poisonous URIC ACID in all cases of small-pox, etc. Even an excess of vegetable protein is injurious.

In malarial diseases we always find an excess of carbonic acid or other acidulous products of decaying or germ inhabited sugars or glycerines (from grease, etc.).

A diet of skim-milk and white bread will cure malaria, and a diet of SKIM-MILK and oat-meal will cure kidney disease.

During health the blood is always ALKALINE, while the tissues or nerves and ganglia or brain are always acidulous. NOW THIS IS WHAT I WANT TO IMPRESS UPON THE MIND, for it relates to my discovery of the WHITE SPARK PRINCIPLE. An acid acts like heat, while an alkali acts like cold. The molecules in an acid are rotating in orbits, while the molecules of an alkali rotate on an axis, so we can see how when the blood becomes acidulous as in disease WHITE SPARK CELLS OF LIFE CANNOT BE FORMED.

SUGAR has proven itself a bane to humanity. It is a modern product and was not used by the ancients. Honey had a limited field as a luxury, and here I will say the high cost of luxuries has been a protective principle for poor people.

Sugar has no limit of solution. Water will absorb it until an immobile syrup is formed, and glycerine, a product of grease, acts similar to sugar in the system.

Syrup has a great affinity for LIME, and children who eat candy and sweet foods have bad teeth, as the lime required for the teeth is absorbed from the blood by the sugar. Any chemist knows the great affinity of syrup for lime, and this is why he makes the syrup of lime which is used in prescriptions where lime is required.

Sugar acts as an acid, chemically, forming Saccarites with the bases or alkalis. Sugar destroys the natural alkaline state of the blood.

There has been a great scare around Boston about a "NEW DISEASE." The doctors have various ideas about its nature and treatment. It is generally called ACIDOSIS and is supposed to be the result of eating too much sugar; but some doctors say it is AN EPIDEMIC and is not caused by sugar. In the disease the blood has been found to be acidulous.

Sugar will fill the system with an embalming element, and thus the tissues are saturated with an element which acts on the system like ashes thrown on a fire. They extinguish it, and as sugar prevents oxidation in the system, the VACO-CELLS or "WHITE SPARKS" cannot form.

There are times when electrical machines will produce only a few weak sparks and at other times powerful sparks are produced, and it has been proved that this state of non-electrical atmosphere is the cause of

EPIDEMICS when the system is loaded with either sugar or gelatinous products of a meat diet.

Fasting is often necessary in disease, for disease is usually a congestion of the blood and a distention of the blood vessels, and when we lessen the quantity of blood or the excessive pressure from the effects of stimulants, etc., we allow the blood vessels to get a grip on the blood and force it along. A dog or horse will never eat when he is sick.

An invalid for a time may do best on a little toasted white bread and skim-milk, as oat-meal, etc., may contain too much gluten, which is not needed in the system at this time. There is a difference in proteins. Gluten is more like gelatin and is used where toughness is required as in the skin, tendons and muscle. The vital proteins are required in the nerves and brain.

It is not well to eat eggs for breakfast in all kinds of sickness, but a soft boiled egg for dinner may be good for some.

The excessive use of meat is a cause of cancer, and it is the gelatin which is to blame. There are two factors, however, which should be considered. We may eat gelatin, sugar or grease, and if we work hard in the open air we overcome the disease in a measure. It has been proved that carnivorous fishes have cancers if the fishes are crowded in a pool, but removal to running water cures them, as running water contains more air and oxygen which gives more nerve power and eliminates the useless material.

It is the same with malaria. Work in the pure air burns off the hydro-carbons better and the blood becomes more mobile.

When we use oat-meal, mush, etc., with skim-milk we don't get much solid food, for we fool ourselves by taking lots of water which we would not use otherwise. In winter stabled horses are seen to excrete dark heavy urine, as they are fed on grain or proteins and drink little water. Vegetables contain much water and are useful.

The air in closed rooms is dead, but out-door air is in motion. Decay and filth fills the air with gasses and oxygen is displaced, which means death to "the white spark" of the nerves, the generators of power.

If you have money and leisure you can dissipate more with less inconvenience than as if you had no money or time.

It has been proved that the use of alcohol, tobacco, etc., wastes the tissues and nourishment the same as hard work and overworks the liver, kidneys and lungs; but work is the poor man's bulwark, and thus it is that the abstemious person is always a better, wiser, more reasonable and industrious employ than the other.

The "sport" has a debauch and then a "loaf" or else he soon goes to the sanitarium. Stimulants always lessen your powers after each dose or after the first effects are worn out.

We can show you how to overcome poverty without a labor union propaganda, or a lodge benefit, for you can live on a few cents per day and become better off thereby, if you follow the right method. Many have tried to live on boiled potatoes, beans, skim-milk and vegetables, but have failed; but the trouble was this: the system had been adapted to the stimulation of creation, the stimulant of meat, and when this was withdrawn there was a slack action to the stomach and general system. But I have proved that if you use some onions or celery or some mild condiment like pepper or the like you can avoid meat without trouble.

Many reformers have failed because they drop stimulants, yet still eat soups and meats or cakes and rich dishes. YOU MUST DROP THESE THINGS WHEN YOU DROP ALCOHOL AND DRUGS, for meat gelatins, grease and sugar make a heavy refractory blood and nature calls for an increased nerve action, but this stimulation is a first stage of inflammation with its weakening reaction. Starch is transformed into grape sugar in the intestines, yet nature regulates this better than when sugar is taken directly into the stomach, as this goes directly to the liver.

The simple living person gets up earlier, works easier and gets more enjoyment from the sunshine, the open fireplace and all the beauties of nature.

A fine cigar may stimulate the brain, but like Emerson you may decline when you should be in your prime, and perhaps, like him, lose your memory. Emerson in his last years attended the funeral of his old friend, Longfellow the poet, but could not remember this man's name at his last rites.

I believe it is utterly impossible for any person to live a real safe moral life, according to the Christian code, and subsist upon the ordinary food and drink of the times. For instance, the use of coffee will often create immoral feelings which a saint could not overcome. Tobacco creates sensations in a like manner. Anything which creates undue nerve action causes a congestion of the inner organs. I might as well tell you to place a torch in a powder magazine and then prevent an explosion as to tell you to become a true Christian and live upon highly exciting foods or drugs.

There was never a true saint which did not practice self-restraint in regard to foods, drinks and habits.

You will see that I am an advocate of the simple life, yet I want to say that I am not trying to drive anyone against their will, and I also want to say that I do not say you will go to immediate destruction, always, by diverging from my creed. Some persons from the nature of their ordinarily proper habits withstand much that is tabooed by science, yet this does not change the facts that correct physiological habits are the only ones to be condoned.

The use of some fruit sauce may not always prove serious, of course, and the farmer who eats baked apples and milk may plod along in his own way and retain good health, yet an invalid who can barely keep alive had better be fed on easily assimilated concentrated life building food. As explained elsewhere, a person who does not use alcohol or tobacco, etc., can use some fruit sauces, etc., and as the poisons have not weakened the nerves which govern the liver and vital organs, the liver can take care of the acids and sugars. Stimulants create wastes in excess and overpower the kidneys and liver, and when they are discarded there is loss of required nerve power.

When a nation has any serious business on hand or when Arctic explorers want to get to their goal they abolish the use of ALCOHOL.

Russia has been under prohibition for the short time of the war, and the decrease of crime has already proved what a monster DRINK has been. In 33 precincts of Moscow for the first half year of 1914 there was an average of 986 criminal cases a month, while for the first temperance month there were only 406. Crime was reduced 54.7 per cent.

Within two weeks after the closing of the wine shops of Russia she felt as if RESURECTED, and it was proved that perfect temperance was possible and that alcohol was not a necessity.

This is only the working out of a Natural Law and is the enactment of one branch of codes, and it holds true of drugs and all of the many branches of physiological requisites.

Individual freedom many times is a menace to a person's welfare. This is proved by the "freedom" with which persons can get drunk.

If the monarch was a wise and conscientious ruler, an absolute monarchy would be a blessing. God is an absolute monarch and his law is absolute. Nature has no favorites and we must obey the law or pay the penalty.

Society is to blame for crime. If municipalities would enact ordinances preventing the dispensing of injurious foods and drinks, and otherwise control the PREVENTION of a person's dissipation, it would necessarily vanish.

But we see the evils of giving legislatures power to enact coercive medical laws when ignorance controls the legislators.

The forcing of citizens to submit to the inoculation of virus or serum in themselves or their animals is equal to the monstrosities of the medieval ages. The recent epidemic of hoof and mouth disease, the Germ Doctors themselves admit, was caused by a hog cholera serum which was tested by the government bacteriologists and pronounced clean and was sold by a Chicago firm. The hoof and mouth disease has never been proved to be a generator of specific "germs," as no microscope has ever detected any such germ, and the poison will pass through a porcelain filter. So how can the virus be "tested?"

There is an epidemic of "Grip" about now, and a health doctor, Dr. Chapin of Providence, R. I., says: "Persons with mild attacks continue at their work and thus rapidly spread the disease. It is for this reason that isolation and official control have never been able to check an outbreak. The epidemics run out themselves after a few weeks."

Well, then, we are safe! Let them run out instead of poisoning thousands of healthy persons with Typhoid and other serums.

Every German soldier, it is claimed, is given the three inoculations of Typhoid Serum before going to the front, but recent medical reports say the Typhoid fever has been malignant in the men in the trenches.

There has recently been a great amount of study about the ductless glands of the animal body. It has been variously claimed this thing and the other for their uses, but I am going to tell what nature made them for, THEY ARE FOR THE REDUCTION OR "DECAY" OF PROTEIDS WHICH MAKES THEM VERY SOLUBLE AND READY FOR THE FEEDING OF THE NERVES AND CELLS. The elements which go into them never come out, but are reabsorbed. With one exception, the male sacs eject the nerve food for the propagation of the species, but it is a cause of disease and weakness.

It is proved that the ductless glands (or sacs) take in proteins which become formed into granules and gradually decay or are broken down enough to be reabsorbed.

The loss of the fluids of these glands is the loss of an alkaline nerve food, and many diseases would be avoided if chastity had been preserved. They prevent the acidity of the blood, which is the cause of many diseases.

The bacteriologists must learn that they cannot fool nature. If your system holds substances which nature must remove by germs it is of no use to kill the germs, because this does not remove the cause. If we kill all the specific germs of one disease, then nature will give some other germs in place of them.

There has been a great cry that consumption has decreased. Perhaps it has, but nature still gives just as much action with her required eliminating process as ever. Here is what Dr. Hutchinson writes in the Boston American, January 10, 1916:

"Although, in the main, the march of modern medicine has been a series of triumphs, at certain points its progress has been checked, if not actually defeated.

"While we have been steadily beating back typhoid, tuberculosis and diphtheria, most of the diseases which have baffled us have been either maladies of later life, like cancer and arterial sclerosis, or conditions depending upon long continued action of a variety of imperfectly known causes, like heart disease, Bright's disease and insanity.

"But there is also one disease among the pure infections whose germ has been identified, whose active cause known for nearly thirty years past, which still defies us, and that is pneumonia.

"In fact, for some ten or fifteen years past, we have been faced with the singular and disquieting paradox, that of the two greatest and most fatal diseases of the lungs, while tuberculosis has been steadily declining, pneumonia has been rapidly increasing in deadliness.

"Twenty years ago tuberculosis caused about one-seventh of all the deaths in the United States; pneumonia, about one-fifteenth. To-day tuberculosis has fallen to about one-twelfth of the deaths, while pneumonia has risen to one-tenth.

"One reason why pneumonia so baffled medical skill was that, although the germ, or rather germs—for there are at least four varieties of them, each producing a different type of the disease—were well known, the infection seldom naturally spreads to other human beings, and it was for a long time rather difficult to transmit it experimentally to animals.

"Further than that, the pneumococcus which produced the most serious types of the disease was, if not identical with, quite hard to distinguish from two or three types of streptococci which were found in abundance in the human mouth, about the roots of the teeth and in the tonsils, even in conditions of perfect health.

"So that we were driven to the discouraged conclusion that some 'state of the system,' or lowered resisting power or other unknown factor, was necessary in order to allow the pneumonia coccus to get a foothold in the lungs and produce the disease; and there the case hung for a number of years.

The Open Air Cure.

"Considerable improvement in all but the most virulent type of cases was produced by the introduction of the open air treatment, with abundant feeding similar to that relied upon in tuberculosis. But we could not honestly say that we knew of any drug or remedy which appeared to have a directly curative effect upon the disease."

Can't you see that the product is 22 in either case? And don't you see that the "germ doctors" have not fooled nature?

There is a great epidemic of "grip" and pneumonia sweeping the country—one of the worst ever known. In Providence, R. I., the disease has been the cause of more deaths in a given time than was ever known. Here is what the Evening Bulletin says in the issue of January 10, 1916:

"Fifteen persons in Providence died of pneumonia or grip during the second half of last week, making 35 lives claimed here by the epidemic in the first eight days of January.

"This is the largest number of deaths from these diseases which the city has ever had in a similar period. Physicians report that there is no indication of a let-up in the epidemic as yet, and that a continuance of the unusually high death rate may be expected.

"There were nine deaths from pneumonia last Thursday, Friday and Saturday, and six fatalities from grip. The deaths for the first eight days of the month are as follows: Pneumonia 24, grip 10, acute bronchitis 1."

At the Rhode Island State Institutions there are nearly 300 cases of the disease—100 at the State Prison alone—but at the State Reform School for girls there is not one case, as this school gives better hygienic care to the inmates. But the great reason is the girls are not dissipated and nature does not have to produce the germs in their systems.

Reformers are often bombarded with statistics by brewery owners, distillers and those whose ideas are regulated by personal benefits. The favorite weapon is the story of the man who lived to be old and always drank or smoked. Here is a reprint of such a story:

HALE AND HEARTY AT 102.
New Jerseyman Chews Tobacco as Preventive of Disease.

Newton, N. J., Dec. 22.—Charles Ashford Shafer, Sushex County's oldest resident, celebrated his one hundred and second birthday at the home of his son, George Shafer, to-day. Mr. Shafer is still active, hale and hearty, and walks several miles a day. He was born a few miles from here and has spent all his life in this section. For many years he conducted a distillery. The centenarian declares that chewing tobacco is a means of preventing disease, and he has been chewing it since a boy. Mr. Shafer reads without the aid of glasses.

But wait a minute—here is a better one:

TEETOTALER DEAD AT 115.

West Virginian Never Tasted Liquor or Tobacco in His Life.

Wheeling, W. Va., Nov. 29.—Henderson Cremeans, known to be the oldest man in West Virginia and probably the oldest in the United States, died to-day at the home of his grandson, Clark Cremeans, near Point Pleasant, Mason County, aged 115 years. He never tasted liquor or tobacco in his life.

And when we study statistics of the insurance business we may rest assured that they are correct, for an insurance company gets a premium on every policy and regulates its action upon the correct statistics. Here is another reprint:

SAYS PROHIBITION IN RUSSIA WILL SAVE 500,000 MEN

Insurance Expert Claims That If Czar Carries Out Present Intention, Loss of Half Million in War Will Be Made Up in Decade.

New York, Dec. 11.—Results of an investigation in which an entirely new set of statistics had been gathered were put before the Association of Life Insurance Presidents at their annual meeting at the Hotel Astor yesterday and threw a new light on the influence of alcoholism, overeating, undereating, and other factors in shortening lives.

The investigation, which has just been completed, concerned the causes of premature deaths in the last 25 years among the 2,000,000 policy holders of 43 leading insurance companies. The object of the investigation was to determine which types of persons could be insured safely at regular rates, which ones should pay extra premiums, and which ones should be refused. The results were given by Arthur Hunter, chairman of the bureau that made the investigation.

"If the Government of Russia carries out its present intention to abolish permanently all forms of alcoholic beverages, the saving in human life will be enormous," said Mr. Hunter. "The loss of 500,000 men as the result of the present warfare could be made good in less than ten years through complete abstinence from alcoholic beverages by all the inhabitants of Russia.

"Among saloon proprietors, whether they attended the bar or not, there was an extra mortality of 70 per cent., and the causes of death indicated that a free use of alcoholic beverages had caused many of the deaths. The hotel proprietors who attended the bar, either occasionally or regularly, had as high a mortality as the saloon keepers.

"Among the men who admitted that they had taken alcohol occasionally to excess in the past, but whose habits were considered satisfactory when they were insured, there were 289 deaths, while there would have been only 190 deaths had this group been made up of insured lives in general. The extra mortality was, therefore, over 50 per cent."

Cardinal Gibbons says: "Reform must come from within," and he opposes prohibition; but there is no question but what prohibition is the right thing as has been proved, for in some persons the only thing "within" is alcohol and ignorance.

SOCIETY is about our only hope. Lord Bacon wrote the first half of a book on this subject of an ideal society or community, and he described as a first requisite his "SOLOMON'S HOUSE," a college or school where NATURAL SCIENCE was taught.

Thomas More portrayed the same ideas in his "UTOPIA," a beautiful island where ideal laws and conditions prevailed. Campanella also had an idea in his "CITY OF THE SUN."

Where temptation is removed better conditions exist, for human nature always wavers and no one is permanently wise. The lad in the country is healthier than the one in the city. Why? Because there are less temptations in the country.

What is it that perfects animals but forcing proper rules upon them?

I have experimented with fowl and found that you can perfect them by proper treatment. I raised 56 pullets one spring, and that winter I had eggs galore. The fowl were healthy and happy. I fed them only two meals a day on cracked corn and wheat or the regular "scratch feed" of the market in the morning, and at night gave them scalded meal, seasoned with some salt, pepper and onions; sometimes cooked potato parings, etc., were used. I supplied the fowl with fresh ground bone which held some fat, of course. I always had gravel and ground oyster shells before them, also plenty of fresh water. They had their run and found grass both in summer and winter, and had a dry, roomy house.

Meat is not only unnecessary to animal life, but is injurious. My hens laid more eggs than any others about and were bright, active and healthy, yet they had no meat during all the winter. The bone was not necessary, for I had at times fed poultry a little fat or oil instead of the ground bone, and they did just as well.

The mind has a great effect on the digestion, and it is necessary in selecting our food and drink to have it agreeable. Of course, this does not mean that because something tastes good we should use it, for poisons often taste pleasant. We mean that from a variety of salutary food we should select what we like, and again any combination, adjustment or preparation which enhances the food is very useful. For instance:

Potatoes mashed, mixed with eggs, flour, pepper and salt and other articles which are not injurious, and then fried in a little butter are very agreeable, and many such manipulations of foods are wise.

But spices, coffee, tea and such condiments contain tannin and poisons and should be eschewed.

If a person should suddenly change his diet from a liberal one to mush and skim-milk it might give him indigestion and disgust, for the organs try to adapt themselves to certain kinds of food; and if the persons cannot take a vacation while reforming their diet, it might be better to wait until they can. After a fit of sickness one can start with the right kind of food and drink and improve by it.

People who are raised on simple food relish it and keep happy and healthy. Here is a reprint which proves this to be true:

"According to census reports, persons who live 100 years or more are very scarce. The United States, with a population of more than 90,000,000, is given credit for only 46. Germany's population is 60,000,000 and its quota of centenarians is 70. Great Britain, with a population of 46,000,000, has 94. France, with 40,000,000, claims 164. Bulgaria, with 4,000,000 inhabitants, boasts of 3,300, and Roumania, with 6,000,000 people, has 3,320 centenarians. The last named little countries eat little meat and use a great deal of milk and dark bread."

The persons who used tobacco, etc., and lived to be old might have lived much longer if they had been abstemious. William Smellie in his "Philosophy of Natural History" records cases where persons have lived to be over 150 years old, and some of the oldest people, for instance, Capt. Diamond, was a simple living man and lived to be 113 (when I last heard from him). He never even used sugar and was an old bachelor, showing that simple life allows continence.

It has been proved that meat allows an alkaloid condition in the intestines which generates poison producing germs, while vegetable food, like oat-meal, etc., produces an acid condition which, it is claimed, "prevents the generation of microbes and poisons which produce premature old age." The large intestine when retaining the elements from the bowels too long becomes a "filth reservoir."

Prof. Metchnikoff says that animals having a greater length to the large intestines do not live as long as those with shorter large intestines, which cannot breed the poisonous bacteria so well, yet he is puzzled by the long life proportionately of the squirrel, which has a long intestine, and he says he has found few of the "dreaded bacteria" in the intestine of the squirrel. (This is because the squirrel has not the noisome elements here which harbor germs.)

The recent discoveries that VEGETABLE food inhibits the generation of the microbes or renders them unnecessary is an object lesson which tells us to live upon the foods as I recommend, for the squirrel lives upon vegetable food or nuts, which are seeds with Vaco-Cell forming molecules.

We need not discard the use of a few condiments of a mild nature from our food, and a little salt, pepper or onion, etc., may not be prohibited.

It has been found that a good regime is made up of a breakfast of skim-milk and well cooked oat-meal; a dinner of boiled potatoes, eggs or fish and boiled rice and skim-milk, and a supper of skim-milk, rice and perhaps boiled beans. If you are not a hard worker you should not use too many beans or any excess of protein foods, and a few boiled onions, etc., may be added to the dinner if desired. A little butter may be used with food if skim-milk is used, but the use of an excess of rich milk loads the blood with too much grease.

The outside hull of grains, beans, peas, etc., contain cellulin, an indigestible woody fibre which acts as a mechanical laxative to the bowels and aids health if you can use coarse food. Of course, invalids could not always use such food, as their stomach can hardly digest milk or eggs. Fruit and acids should not be used as foods by invalids.

The germ of grain and seeds in general is a great nerve food or "spark generator," but as it is highly organized it changes easily and so is not used in fine flour.

My theory is that the whole universe is interdependent and that there can be no separation of its component parts. We and all things are joined together the same as a knitted sock—joined by invisible lines of force; and as all matter is simply a peculiar aspect or motion of spirit or the ether, and as no part of the ether can be separated or absolutely isolated, it is an axiom that the universe is ONE. Nothing can be moved except there is a fulcrum. It may be infinitesimal or like an isthmus though.

The great scientists are now admitting this to be a fact. Prof. Edgar Lucien Larkin says: "In the ultimate, what distinction can be drawn between organic and inorganic matter, since mind is matter or force? Therefore, is it not but matter or force under a different aspect or relation to surrounding appearances, or, in other words, are not all things a unit?"

This scientist further says: "The ultimate distinction between inorganic and organic matter is the inscrutable mystery." And here is where I am able to explain this GREAT MYSTERY.

LIFE is spirit and I have discovered a process in Nature, which we explain in other works more extensively, by which she forms invisible "VACUUM

CELLS" in matter, which are conscious and with a potential of radio-activity, and this is the principle of all life and form in organic bodies and in the snow-flake, etc. The process is simple and is from alternations of heat and cold.

In the bioplasmic foods of nature the germ of seeds, for instance, we find a peculiar arrangement of the molecules. They contain a cell center of SOLUBLE SULPHUR, SILICON OR PHOSPHORUS. This arrangement facilitates the formation of the white spark, and the formation of this wonderful food in plants depends upon the soil.

Alkali, and carbonic acid gas, in the nascent state, makes SULPHUR, SILICON, Phosphorus and IRON soluble. I have evaporated five gallons of spring water and obtained the solid residue and found out the wonderful nature of the cell center elements. These minerals are hydrated and at a temperature of 100 degrees they are liquids, and at 50 degrees they are solids. This explains the reason why certain protein foods are "bioplasmic" and how easily the white sparks are generated in the nerves and brain. The bodily or tissue temperature when life is active is 100 degrees and the oxygenized blood and evaporation from the lungs and skin reduces the temperature of the molecules to 50 and the life vacuo are formed. Oxygenized blood cells are discs rotating on an axis like an alkali.

I have in other publications explained that meat was a second-hand food, in which many life molecules were exploded (gelatin), and that the protein portions of milk, eggs and vegetable foods contained "CARTRIDGES OF LIFE AND POWER," that is, molecules having sulphur or phosphorus centers which under proper conditions formed VACO-CELLS, especially the germ of all seeds which is absent in fine flour usually.

I discovered the paradox of temperatures by accident. I had been in correspondence with Sir William Crookes, President of the British Association for the

Advancement of Science in England, and in connection with a scientific matter he had advised me to evaporate the water of a certain Spring, and it was in following out his directions that I found "THE CENTER FORMING MOLECULAR ELEMENTS," which nature uses in forming foods.

There have been many changes in the ideas of scientists within a few years. Several years ago I was taken to task for stating that the wave lengths of a line of force could be shortened or increased by the nature of the substance which it passed through, but one of the Great Professors—Garrett P. Serviss—has just stated: "So the waves of radiant energy sent out from the sun are not heat, but have been set going by heat in the sun and CAN BE TRANSFORMED into heat again on encountering the earth."

Anyone may perform two interesting experiments which prove the statements which I make in regard to "the white spark."

When the soldering compound which is sold to fill up holes in marbleized iron ware is melted and dropped into cold water, peculiar little bodies are formed—little rubber bags or cells filled with powdered sulphur at the center; the compound being composed of sulphur, rubber and quicksilver in this experiment follows the natural laws, and the opposite features of heat conduction causes the sulphur to be encased with the more organic rubber.

The other experiment is dropping melted tinsmith's solder into water at a temperature of 75 degrees when hollow balls are formed, if care is taken in dropping the metal in a globule.

The great provisions of Nature are so sufficient and magnificent that it is proved that the worriments of mankind are imaginary, and it is a fact that they are the result of physical disorders brought about by improper food, drink and habits.

When I see the beautiful sunshine pouring life-giving rays upon everyone and every atom in the world, when

I see the grandeur and stable travel of the bodies of the sidereal system, when I see the unperturbed growth of the trees, plants and grains, the gentle rain and the whispering winds, I can say surely the human acts of greed, malice and crime are the results of a distorted mind.

Judge Swann says FIFTY per cent. of those who are brought to trial in the criminal courts of New York City are addicted to the use of narcotics.

Judge Collins says that since the "BOYLAN LAW" allows the sale of medicines containing a certain percentage of narcotics, the Health Department cannot pass laws restricting such sales without contradicting the state statutes.

Coffee, tea and other insidious poisons are agents of the "DEVIL" also. Chocolate and roasted wheat, peanuts, etc., are poisonous. Roasting often creates empyrean oil.

It is the ascetics or those who live upon vegetable foods, milk and eggs with some fish, or those who do not overeat and live the "SIMPLE LIFE," who look upon the grandeur of Nature properly and ignore the contingencies of life which others commit suicide over or ply the cry of incongruity in Nature.

Consider the religious martyrs of the medieval ages and see how the little "Jap" with his ration of rice went to battle without fear and endured hardships and put the Russian Army beneath his feet.

It is the same with the abstemious prize fighter. He has more coolness and endurance than the beef steak eater and libertine, as proved by Freddy Welsh, the world's champion lightweight.

The Harvard Football Squad had a number of men stricken with appendicitis after training upon a meat diet, supposing that meat was a requisite to hard work, a fallacy too often disproved.

Jess Willard, the world's champion pugilist, says he never smoked nor drank liquor in his life, and at the end of the battle with Johnson he felt as if he could fight "a thousand rounds."

We all wish PEACE, HAPPINESS, HEALTH, STRENGTH and SUCCESS. The only differences between us are HOW TO OBTAIN THESE DESIRES, and yet a little candid observation will show us the truth.

The first transaction must be a determination and an agreement to become independent of all other codes and methods except those by which the above objects can be attained.

There are many habits which appeal to us as being a means of personal well being, and yet they are insidious enemies.

It is the regime which has a reaction for our health and happiness which we should follow, and we must have sense enough to eschew the methods which are sure to bring a subsequent disaster to us, even if they may induce a temporary pleasure, for there can be but one correct path which leads to elysian joys.

Nature is wiser than we are and we must not set ourselves up as her superiors, for if we do we are sure to fall. We must not make use of her productions until she has finished them, and we must not use things for food or drink which she has arranged for some other purpose. Sugar is an unfinished product of nature, and leaves, barks, etc., containing poisons are not intended for our consumption, and we should not breathe smoke into our lungs when it is intended that only pure air should pass into them.

We should not entertain passion for passion's sake when it was intended only for reproduction. Secretions in ductless and sac filling glands are for reabsorption. If I take the finished products of nature and undo them again, I am as unwise as if I used them before nature finished them. The breweries take the beautiful grains and degenerate them and people use the liquid poisons and do not realize that they are insulting nature and ruining themselves. We take grains, etc., and roast or burn them into poisons and seduce ourselves with the mistaken idea that we are using harmless and innocent food or drink.

We steal the property of others, we extort from them, we are jealous of them with the delusion that we are the benefitted parties, but nothing is more untrue than this idea.

All of the mental, social and physical effects of greed, malice and immorality are indelibly disastrous to us, and we have a mistaken idea of our needs and of the things which make happiness.

What the European War Has Demonstrated.

We have previously stated that FOUR HOURS labor per day was enough for any one, and this would carry on the world's industry adequately and to prove this we give an excerpt from an article by the great English Divine—Rev. R. J. Campbell, his statistics prove that POVERTY IS UNNECESSARY and that wage earners can be paid enough to buy what they wish to make happiness—, pianos and other so-called luxuries, and automobiles could of course be substituted for pianos if their desires should require such.

At the present price of automobiles they are within reach of the man who will give up drinking and using tobacco or other narcotics and I want to say that I believe riding in one of the new type steel bodied automobiles with a magneto ignition is a great health augmenter as these cars when running become charged with electricity and I quite often get a shock from one of my automobiles if I happen to touch part of my hand to the body of the car while the other part has hold of the side shift lever. This statical electricity has been proved by Dr. W. J. Morton, of New York City, to be a wonderful therapeutical agency. When properly supplied to the body it causes the blood discs to take up more oxygen from the air and augments the power of the vital apparatus. (See his address published in the November, 1893, Transactions of the American Institute of Electrical Engineers.)

Riding in a carriage or car will aid the circulation of the body fluids without waste of our own energy, the motions massage the body, the same as muscular action.

Work is a benefit to us but how much do we need is a question,—a sick person can not work and a person's training and condition must regulate this,—too much work draws the vital force from the vital organs and mental work is absolutely injurious in sickness, the brain draws on the vitality to the detriment of the vital organs of the body, yet again the cultivated mind has a power to govern the base faculties which debilitate the body.

Part of the English Divine's Article Which We Have Referred to:

"One of the strangest paradoxes about this period of destructiveness through which we are passing is that there is very little dire poverty about. It has taught me a lesson, a lesson which probably the workers as a class are assimilating too, namely, that destitution and the degradation which so generously accompanies it **could be got rid of in a month** in time of peace if we were only in earnest to do it.

"It is caused simply by an unfair distribution of wealth. We always knew that, but what we did not know was that it could be so speedily remedied. We thought it would take a long time even if the nation were willing to tackle the problem seriously, which it has not yet shown any anxiety to do. We were afraid of drastic experiments of a social nature, with the consequent displacement of capital, the shock given to that very delicate entity, the national credit, and so on.

"Go more slowly, was the universal cry. Give us breathing space. These drastic changes one after the other—all in the direction of making the rich pay more into the pockets of the poor—are very dangerous. You are impairing public confidence; do wait awhile before you attempt anything further. You are imposing a tax on industry which is certain to hinder productiveness.

"And we were wrong, the whole lot of us—Kaiser, German Bureau, British Tories, hesitant Liberals, landowners, bankers, manufacturers, shopkeepers, taxpayers generally, and probably the proletariat, too. It is nothing short of amazing. Here we are hurling our accumulated stores of wealth into hell, the hell of war, and the workers as a whole were never so well off.

"We are able to pay, and we do pay, without complaining. We are doing it without suffering very greatly, without hearing the cry of hunger going up from our congested areas as it has too often done in time of peace, and without the slightest apprehension that we are drawing near to the end of our strength.

"We shall be able to go on doing it for years if need be. The savings of the working classes have hardly yet been touched for national purposes, and if report speaks true there has been a not too creditable increase in the purchase of cheap luxuries—and luxuries not commonly accounted cheap, too, such as pianos—among a section of these, unskilled laborers especially. They are not unpatriotic, but is it to be wondered at that they should suddenly feel themselves well-to-do and fail to realize that war is economic wastage as well as wholesale murder?

"'Three pounds a week, and no 'usband!' a lady engaged in munition work is credited with saying—'Wy, it's 'eaven!' There is humor in the sentiment, one must confess, though it was not complimentary to the absent husband.

"We have withdrawn not less than four million men from productive occupations and set them to smash and kill instead.

"Think of it! And then remember that those men have to be equipped and maintained somehow or other by the rest of us, and that most of them are the very pick of the country's early manhood. And we can afford to do it! We can do it, and in the process make an end of destitution for the time being and secure to wage-earners a higher standard of comfort than they have ever enjoyed before.

"Will the electors of Great Britain, rich and poor, try to digest that fact and grasp its implications? The logic of it is that we can if and when we choose get rid forever of the crying disgrace of starvation and misery at one end of the social scale and senseless ostentation at the other.

"The thing is demonstrated now.

"The army as it exists to-day is a fine all-around leveler. A good many artificial prejudices and social distinctions are being swept away by the power of actual daily comradeship in the face of death. These four million citizen soldiers have votes. How will they use them when they come home?

"Let the lesson be driven well home. We can do all that is required if we want to do it. Behold the economic miracle of to-day, and consider what is possible to-morrow. There need never be another hungry mouth. No honest man ought to have to dread the loss of a job or to lower his self-respect by seeking the aid of the Poor law.

"It is all nonsense to say that the problem of destitution is unsolvable or that our resources will not bear the institution of a standard living wage for everybody and not for the aristocracy of labor only.

"After the debacle of 1871 France was apparently ground to powder, her manhood decimated, her trade ruined, her treasury empty, and an enormous indemnity to pay to her triumphant foe. She recovered so quickly and completely, to the surprise of everybody, that in 1875 Bismarck, like the bully he was, wanted to hit her again, and would have done so but for Queen Victoria and the British Government."

I have shown how to rise above poverty even when the capitalists grind the worker down to a wage inadequate to his service, yet this is not a just condition, and when the war in Europe is over many workers will be back to their countries, to work. There may be lack of employment then, but let the FOUR HOURS per day schedule be put in operation and let the pay be proper and all will be well.

Let the capitalist adjust himself to the fact that the worker is HIS BROTHER and that THEOCRATIC DEMOCRACY is God's Law.

The air, the water and all necessities are one man's as much as another's.

The Kaiser, King George or the President of France must drink the same water which his lowly brother has once drank and breathe the same air which he has breathed.

A King has water brought to him—it may be that this water,—the very identical molecules, were once in the blood and body of a lowly tiller of the soil; he may have drank it, excreted it, it went to the river, to the ocean, then evaporated to the mountain top, and was again precipitated to the earth and leached into the King's well.

The VOTERS HAVE THE POWER TO ADJUST THE LAW; if they belie themselves who is to blame?

Let them institute the INITIATIVE AND REFERENDUM AND THE RECALL OF JUDGES first, then make the proper laws to raise man to the social position where he belongs.

It is well known that much of the poverty and misery of the world has been caused by ALCOHOL, and the use of narcotics is also not far behind in the cause of degradation and misery.

The prohibition laws which have been instituted in Russia prove these statements to be correct and to show the wonderful prosperity which ensues from temperance. I give a statement from Russian Minister of Finance Bark. He says:

"On the other hand, there is nothing illusory or specious about the Russians' prosperity. It rests upon the incontrovertible fact of the Russian people's increased earnings and savings.

"When, a year ago, the savings banks showed a monthly increase of 50,000,000 rubles, it was regarded as phenomenal. But that was only the beginning. During the month of January the savings banks alone showed an increase in deposits of 120,000,000 rubles. This is accounted for principally by the growing thrift and economy of the peasants since the enforcement of prohibition, by their greater earning power and the higher wages they command. This marvelous prosperity makes Russia capable of raising large numbers of successful internal loans, and it is by this means chiefly that we hope to defray the expenses of the war, which have now reached 1,000,000,000 rubles monthly."

Blessings often come to us masquerading as evil; this terrible war has its benefits. While death must come to everyone sometime, it may be that we put too much stress on the fact that so many lives have been sent to the BETTER SHORE within such a short space of time, and it is best to believe in the axiom THAT WHAT IS—IS RIGHT.

There probably will never be another war, and perhaps, it must be that this one is the lever to throw THE "DEVIL" into OBLIVION.

The Germans have seen the revelations as well as the other belligerents. Here is what a writer in Berlin says:

"On Tuesday and Friday there is no meat to be had. On Monday and Thursday the consumption of fats is forbidden. Some alcoholic drinks are forbidden to be sold after 9 o'clock at night. They are mostly liqueurs.

"The enforced abstinence from meat on two days of the week has been accepted everywhere with personal satisfaction. You agree with the German when he tells you that he has eaten too much meat all his life, and is glad the government has made him reform. So on these days he eats fish, oysters and vegetables, and declares he feels the better for it."

This item from Augustus Baech is illuminating and instructive. Grease is not a colloid; it does not absorb the gastric juice like a better organized element, and thus the stomach is irritated. There is a law of Nature by which the molecules affect matter; crystalline substances in solution are readily drawn into colloids. A system of symbols helps understanding in the matter—let us represent an acid by a perpendicular line, an alkali by a horizontal line, a crystal by a pyramid and a colloid by a globule; flat surfaces oppose round ones and a confusion of straight forces would produce a spiral force.

There is a great law of HUMAN BROTHERHOOD, yes, more than that—a law of the brotherhood of all animal life.

The hatred of the English, Germans and Russians in this flaming war of passion is wrong—let us remember St. Peter's vision of the basket let down from heaven with all kinds of men in it.

The reform of diet and habits will relieve the tension of malice, hatred and jealousy, the lessened rage of sexual passion will curtail the undue birth rate, the nations will not need to conquer more territory and the social conditions will be adjusted.

How beautiful would it be to see all men living in peace, harmony, prosperity and happiness.

Let us regain our reason and settle down to truth and common sense and have peace and correct understanding between individuals and nations. IT CAN BE DONE, and THIS WILL BE THE MILLENNIUM.

www.ingramcontent.com/pod-product-compliance
Lightning Source LLC
LaVergne TN
LVHW051846080426
835512LV00018B/3095